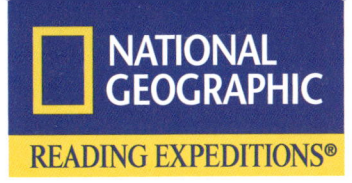

AMERICAN FOLKTALES

Folktales of the Southwest

By Paul Robert Walker
Illustrated by Steve Angel

PICTURE CREDITS
5 (maps) National Geographic Society; 7, 19, 33, 47 illustrations by Ken Cox; 56 © Trevor Wood/Getty Images

PUBLISHED BY THE NATIONAL GEOGRAPHIC SOCIETY
Produced through the worldwide resources of the National Geographic Society, John M. Fahey, Jr., President and Chief Executive Officer; Gilbert M. Grosvenor, Chairman of the Board.

PREPARED BY NATIONAL GEOGRAPHIC SCHOOL PUBLISHING
Sheron Long, Chief Executive Officer; Samuel Gesumaria, President; Francis Downey, Vice President and Publisher; Richard Easby, Editorial Manager; Anne M. Stone, Editor; Margaret Sidlosky, Director of Design and Illustrations; Jim Hiscott, Design Manager; Cynthia Olson, Ruth Ann Thompson, Art Directors; Matt Wascavage, Director of Publishing Services; Lisa Pergolizzi, Production Manager.

MANUFACTURING AND QUALITY CONTROL
Christopher A. Liedel, Chief Financial Officer; Phillip L. Schlosser, Vice President; Clifton M. Brown III, Director.

CONSULTANT
Mary Anne Wengel

BOOK DESIGN
Artful Doodlers and Insight Design Concepts Ltd.

"Pecos Bill Finds a Ranch but Loses a Wife" © 1993, 2006 Paul Robert Walker. All other stories and "Story Behind" sections © 2006 Paul Robert Walker.

Copyright © 2007 National Geographic Society. All Rights Reserved. Reproduction of the whole or any part of the contents without written permission is prohibited. National Geographic, National Geographic Reading Expeditions, and the Yellow Border are registered trademarks of the National Geographic Society.

Published by the National Geographic Society
1145 17th Street N.W.
Washington, D.C. 20036-4688

Product #4U1005096
ISBN: 978-1-4263-5089-4

Printed in Mexico

11 10 09 08 07
10 9 8 7 6 5 4 3 2 1

BIOGRAPHY / ACKNOWLEDGMENTS
"Pecos Bill Finds a Ranch but Loses a Wife" appeared in similar form in *Big Men, Big Country* by Paul Robert Walker (San Diego: Harcourt Brace Jovanovich, 1993.) Both versions are based on "The Saga of Pecos Bill" by Edward O'Reilly, in Century Magazine 106 (October 1923), reprinted in *A Treasury of American Folklore*, edited by B.A. Botkin (New York: Bonanza Books, 1983.)

"The Turkey Girl" is based on "The Poor Turkey Girl" in *Zuñi Folk Tales*, by Frank Hamilton Cushing (New York: G.P. Putnam's Sons, 1901. Reprint with new introduction. New York: A.A. Knopf, 1931. Reprint. Tucson: University of Arizona Press, 1986.)

"The Flower of Life" is based on "Jovita and Manuelito" by Riley Aiken in *A Good Tale and a Bonnie Tune*, Publications of the Texas Folklore Society, Number XXXII, edited by Mody C. Boatright (Dallas: Southern Methodist University Press, 1964.) Reprinted in *Mexican Folktales from the Borderland*, by Riley Aiken (Dallas: Southern Methodist University Press, 1980.)

"Running with the Mustangs" is based on "Running with the Wild Mares" in *The Mustangs* by J. Frank Dobie (Boston: Little Brown, 1952. Reprint. Austin: University of Texas Press, 1984.)

Folktales of the Southwest

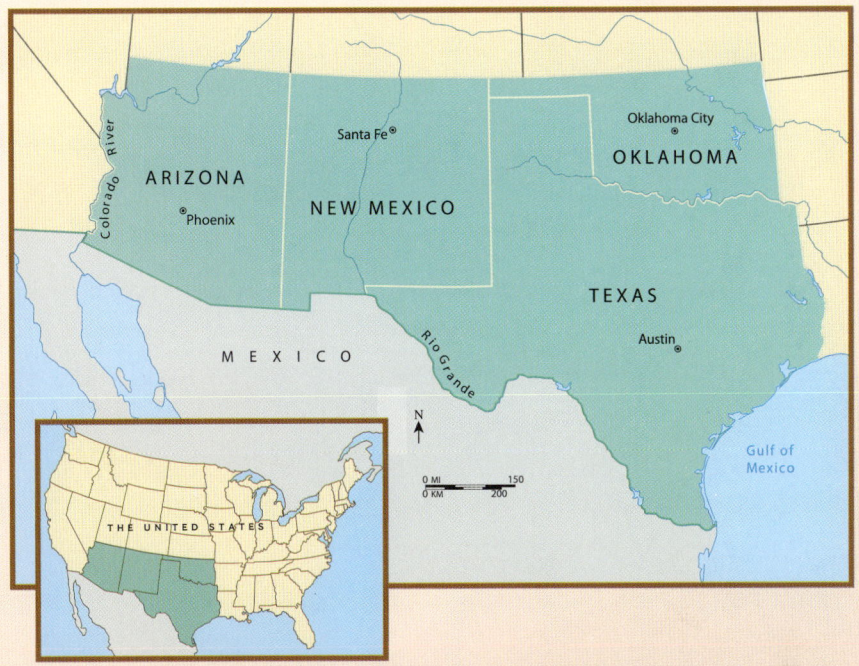

There are many folktales from the U.S. In this book you will read folktales of the Southwest. This region stretches from the plains of Texas to the colorful deserts and mountains of New Mexico and Arizona. Deep canyons and flat topped hills called mesas are two land features of the Southwest. See how many land features you can find as you read the stories.

Tall Tale

Pecos Bill Finds a Ranch but Loses a Wife

Pecos Bill was a cowboy at the age most folks are learning to tie their shoes. Of course Bill didn't wear shoes. He wore boots, a big Stetson hat, and a blue bandanna. He wore chaps to protect his legs, just like all cowboys. But Bill's chaps carried half the dust in west Texas.

They called him Pecos Bill because he fell out of the family wagon when he was a baby and landed in the Pecos River. He was rescued by coyotes, who raised him as one of their own. Bill thought he was a coyote until he saw himself in the river. He was kind of disappointed at first. He liked being a coyote. But he figured the closest thing to being a coyote was being a cowboy. Of course he still liked to howl at the moon.

More than anything, Bill wanted to start a ranch of his own. Most of the land in Texas was fenced in and spoken for. So he rode west into New Mexico. Bill thought it was the nicest looking land he ever saw. He built a fence around the whole state for a ranch. Now, all he needed was a few good men to work the ranch.

Bill was riding around aimlessly when he ran into an old gold miner.

"Tell me, old timer," he asked. "Have you seen any good cowhands? The kind of cowhands who eat beans for dinner, swallow prairie dogs for dessert, and use barbed wire to pick their teeth!"

The old miner took one look at Bill and saw that he wasn't your ordinary rancher. "Sure thing," he said. "There's a bunch of rough customers camping out about two hundred miles down this here wash. But I gotta warn you. They're tough hombres."

"That's what I'm looking for," said Bill. He rode down the wash feeling pretty good. Then, after a hundred miles or so, his horse got scared by something on the trail. It reared up on its hind legs, and Bill held onto the saddle horn for all he was worth. Then the strap broke, and the saddle slipped right down the horse's back, taking Bill with it. The horse ran up the wash, leaving Bill alone on the trail with nothing but a saddle.

Bill got downright peevish when he saw what had spooked his horse. There was a ten-foot rattlesnake in the middle of the trail shaking those rattles and asking for a fight. Bill set his saddle down. Then he started beating the poison out of that big rattlesnake until the poor miserable reptile begged for mercy.

"Please, Bill," said the rattler. "I was just fooling around. I wasn't looking for a real fight."

"You haven't seen a real fight," said Bill. He picked up the snake and slung his saddle over his shoulder. Then he walked down the wash, twirling the rattlesnake like a **lariat** and looping a few gila monsters just to pass the time.

After about forty miles or so, a mountain lion jumped down from a cliff and landed right on Bill's neck, biting away with all the strength he

---

lariat – a rope with a loop used to catch cattle

could muster. It was a good-size mountain lion, too. A little bigger than three cows and a calf.

Bill chuckled to himself and set his saddle and snake on the ground. Then he fought that mountain lion until the fur was flying so thick that it blocked the sun up and down the wash. In about two-and-a-half minutes the mountain lion got down on its knees and apologized. "Sorry, Bill," said the lion. "Can't you take a joke?"

"I can take a joke," said Bill. "What I can't take is walking." So Bill set his saddle on the back of the mountain lion and tied the strap good and tight. Then he picked up the rattlesnake and rode on down the wash, whooping and hollering and having a good old time. Things went a little faster after that, with Bill using the rattlesnake for a whip and riding that big mountain lion a hundred feet at a step.

When he found the camp of the tough hombres, Bill rode right up to the chuck wagon, twirling his rattler and letting loose with a couple of bloodcurdling war whoops. He jerked back on the mountain lion, climbed on down, and hung the snake around his neck. Then he grabbed ten or twenty handfuls of hot beans, swallowed a few

prairie dogs, and washed it all down with a couple gallons of boiling coffee. When he was full he wiped his face on a prickly pear cactus.

"Who's the boss around here?" he asked.

A tough-looking hombre walked up to Bill. He was about eight feet tall and weighed three hundred pounds. He had pistols and bullets and knives strapped all over his chest. He looked Bill up and down, and spoke kind of meek and polite and careful. "I was the boss," he said, "but I ain't about to argue with a man who rides a mountain lion, twirls a rattlesnake, and uses a cactus for a napkin. You're the boss, now—boss."

Bill nodded at the giant hombre and took a look at the men. They were a rough, tough-looking bunch, sitting around the campfire and picking their teeth with barbed wire. That old miner was right. They were just the men he needed. Twirling his rattlesnake, Bill hopped on the back of his mountain lion and waved his hat in the air. "C'mon, boys!" he roared. "I got a little ranch I call New Mexico!"

With his new cowhands, Bill had the ranch working in no time. He put the giant hombre in charge of the cattle, and he looked after the horses himself. One little colt really caught Bill's eye. He was pure black and full of fire from the minute he stood on four legs. Bill named him Widow-Maker and raised him on cactus and dynamite. Normally Bill wouldn't let other people near Widow-Maker—for their own safety, of course. But he made one exception and he never forgave himself.

You see Bill was always popular with the ladies, but he only fell in love once. The gal's name was Slue-Foot Sue. Slue-Foot means her feet turned out to the sides, kind of like a penguin. That made it hard to walk. But Sue made up for her walking problems by being the greatest rider in the West. Except for Bill, of course.

Bill first saw Sue riding a catfish on the Rio Grande. In those days Rio Grande catfish were about as big as whales, so Bill was mighty love-struck. Sue was just as moony over Bill. They decided to get married as soon as she could get herself a proper wedding dress.

Back then all the ladies' dresses had big, wide skirts. Some had big steel-spring bustles under the skirt to make them stick out behind. The bustles looked kind of like a giant slinky! When Sue's dress arrived it had the biggest bustle a dress could have. She slipped right into it, and Bill dusted off his boots. The wedding was the wildest party west of the Pecos River!

In the middle of all the whooping and celebrating, Sue turned to Bill and asked, "Honey, can I ride your horse?"

"Now darling," said Bill, "you know I don't let anyone ride Widow-Maker."

"But you've seen me ride a catfish," Sue replied. "Besides, I'm your wife. What's yours is mine and what's mine is yours."

Well Slue-Foot Sue was such a beautiful bride that Bill's tough old heart got kinda soft and mushy. "Okay," he said. "Just this once."

Sue ran right over to Widow-Maker and hopped on, wedding dress and all. Widow-Maker flashed Bill a "what-do-you-think-you're-doing" kind of look. He started to buck and bronc and buck some more. Anyone else would've been thrown with the first few bucks, but Slue-Foot Sue was an expert rider and she hung on tight.

That got Widow-Maker even angrier, so he bucked and bronced again. This time it was

serious bucking and broncing. The ground shook and cracked all the way down to the Rio Grande. Finally, Widow-Maker threw Slue-Foot Sue so high she had to duck to avoid hitting her head on the moon!

When Sue stopped going up, she started coming down faster and faster until she was streaking like a comet. She hit the ground, bounced on that big steel-spring bustle, and went flying up again, higher than before. About a half hour later, she came down and bounced again, flying even higher. This went on and on, with Sue flying higher after every bounce.

Bill stood all mopey and sorrowful, watching his bouncing bride and feeling completely helpless. He watched for a couple of weeks, until the bounces started coming every other day. Then he mounted Widow-Maker and rode away. Most folks think Slue-Foot Sue is still bouncing somewhere up around Jupiter.

Bill never really recovered from the loss of Slue-Foot Sue. He always had a sorrowful expression on his face, and he just plain refused to laugh. The truth is old Pecos Bill was pretty darn miserable.

Then one day, he met a fella from back East. He was wearing a mail-order cowboy suit with shiny spangles and nice clean chaps that never saw a speck of range dust. The Eastern dude cornered Bill and started asking him silly questions about the West, like "Where's Texas?" and "Do rattlesnakes really rattle?"

At first Bill tried to be polite and answer the fella's questions as if they were almost reasonable. But after about forty-seven questions the Eastern dude tipped back his mail-order cowboy hat, pushed out his shiny spangled chest, and said, "Yep, I guess I'm a real cowboy now."

That was too much. Bill smiled a little and then he smiled a little more. And then he laughed—and laughed some more. He laughed a little harder and harder still, until pretty soon he was laughing so hard he could barely breathe. Finally, he just lay down in the dust of New Mexico and plain laughed himself to death.

The Story Behind This Tall Tale

This is a tall tale, a story in which characters and events are exaggerated. Some tall tale heroes were real people, including Davy Crockett and John Henry. Others are made up by storytellers. These characters include Paul Bunyan and Pecos Bill. Bill's wife, Slue-Foot Sue, is also a made-up character.

From the early days of riding the range, cowboys told stories around the campfire. Some of these stories were tall tales. The hero was usually a local cowboy or the person who was telling the story. It is possible that cowboys began to tell stories about Pecos Bill around a hundred years ago. But we don't know for sure.

The first written story about Pecos Bill was published in a magazine in 1923. It was written by a man named Edward O'Reilly. After O'Reilly's story, other writers also wrote stories about Pecos Bill. Some experts believe that O'Reilly made up the story completely. Others think he heard some of the ideas from old cowboys. My tale is based on O'Reilly's original story.

Native American Tale

The Turkey Girl

Long ago, the Native Americans of the Southwest did not have horses or sheep or cattle. Instead they had large flocks of turkeys. The wealthy people would hire the poorest people to take care of their turkeys. So it was at the village of Salt City, in the shadow of Thunder Mountain—near what is now the border of New Mexico and Arizona.

Among the turkey herders was a young girl with no family and few possessions. She lived in a tiny house with a single room. Her clothes were little more than rags. She had a pleasant face and bright shining eyes. But no one paid attention to her, because they saw only a poor girl in dirty clothing. She received nothing for her work except a small amount of food.

Every day the girl released the turkeys from their cages and herded them on the plains around Thunder Mountain. The turkeys loved the girl, for she was always kind to them. They would always come when she called them.

One day, the girl drove her turkeys down near a bigger city called Zuni. Everyone in the city was excited because a dance would be held in four days. It was the Dance of the **Sacred** Bird. This is a very special dance, especially for young people. It is a dance where the young girls are invited to dance with the young men.

The Turkey Girl had never been to a dance. She had never even been allowed to watch a dance. "Oh, I would love to go to this dance," she said out loud. "But it is impossible. I could not even watch in these poor rags."

For the next three days, she herded her turkeys as usual. She could see the people of Salt City preparing their finest clothing and special

sacred – something that is shown great respect

foods for the dance. They laughed and talked about the big event. Since she spent so much time alone with her turkeys, she often spoke to them. She told them how much she wished she could go to the dance. Then, each night, she brought them back to their cages on the outside of the village.

On the fourth day, all the people of Salt City went to Zuni for the Dance of the Sacred Bird. The Turkey Girl sadly watched them walk down the trail. Then she continued to herd her turkeys on the plains.

Male turkeys are called gobblers. Suddenly one of the big gobblers, walked right up to Turkey Girl. He spread out his tail like a fan and puffed out his wings. He stretched his neck as if he were very important. Then he began to speak!

"Maiden Mother, we know your thoughts, and we pity you. Surely you are as worthy to attend the dance as the other people of Salt City. If you take us into our cages very early this afternoon, we will make sure that you have the finest clothing. You will look so beautiful that all the young men will ask where you came from. They will be eager to take your hand and dance with you in the circle."

At first the Turkey Girl was amazed that the gobbler could speak. But as she thought of all the time she had spent with her turkeys, it did not seem so strange. "Oh my beloved turkeys," she said. "I am so happy that we can talk. But why do you speak of this dance? You know how much I want to go. And you know it is impossible."

"Trust in us," said the gobbler. "I speak your language and the language of my people. When we begin to call to each other, follow us home. We will show you what we can do for you. Remember this. We wish for you to enjoy the dance. In return you must not forget us, your friends. If you forget us, then you are just like the people who forget you. We will say, 'Our Maiden Mother deserves the hard life she leads.' But if you remember us, there is no limit to the joys that await you."

The Turkey Girl did not believe the turkeys could really do all that the gobbler promised. But she could not imagine forgetting her turkey friends. "Oh turkeys!" she cried. "I will never forget you. If you tell me what to do, I will obey you, just as you have always obeyed me."

Very early that afternoon, the turkeys began to head home without being told to go by the Turkey Girl. They all knew their places and filed into their cages. Then the big gobbler spoke: "Enter our house, Maiden Mother." She did as he ordered, walking into the turkey cage. "Now sit and give us your garments one by one. We will make them like new."

The Turkey Girl took off the ragged mantle that she wore around her shoulders. She set it on the ground before the gobbler. He took it in his beak and spread it out fully. He pecked and pecked at it. He walked back and forth on it, opening and closing his wings. Then he picked it up again in his beak and walked in a circle. He puffed and puffed. Finally, he laid the garment at her feet. It was now a beautiful white mantle, with elegant designs sewn into it!

The Turkey Girl gazed in delight at the beautiful mantle. Another big gobbler came forward, and she gave him another piece of clothing. He, too, worked his turkey magic.

Then another gobbler stepped up, and another, and another. Soon all her clothes were

as beautiful as any clothing in Salt City. Perhaps even more beautiful than any clothing in Zuni.

    Before the Turkey Girl put on her new garments, she stood in the center of the cage. All the turkeys danced around her, singing and clucking and brushing her with their wings. Soon her body was clean, and her skin was as smooth and shiny as the fairest maidens of the wealthiest families. Her hair was soft and wavy. Her cheeks were full. Her eyes danced with joy. Now she saw that the turkeys could do all that they promised.

One old turkey came forward and said, "You are as fair as any maiden. You are only missing the rich jewels and ornaments that the wealthy maidens wear. Wait a moment. We have sharp eyes and we often find small, precious things that are dropped by careless humans."

The old turkey spread his wings and began to walk around the cage. He threw his head back, letting his long beard rest on his neck. Then he began to cough and a beautiful necklace appeared in his beak!

Another turkey coughed up a pair of earrings. Others coughed up rings and other precious things. Finally, all the ornaments that a wealthy maiden wore in those days were laid at the feet of the Turkey Girl.

She decorated herself with these beautiful things and thanked the turkeys many times for their magic. As she began to leave for the dance, the big gobbler cried out: "Oh Maiden Mother, leave the gate open. For who knows if you will remember your turkeys now that your fortune is changed? Perhaps you will be ashamed that you were once a Turkey Girl. We love you and wish you only happiness. But remember your promise and do not stay too long at the dance. You must be home by sunset."

With a final promise to return by sunset, the Turkey Girl left the gate open and walked down toward Zuni. When she arrived, many handsome young men and beautiful maidens were dancing in the great circle. As soon as the Turkey Girl entered the **plaza,** the eyes of the audience turned away from the dancers and looked at the

---

plaza – an open space in the center of a town

new arrival. "Who is this beautiful maiden?" they asked. "Where did she come from? "Why have we not seen her before?"

She did not stand alone for long. The chiefs of the dance quickly rushed to her and apologized that everything was not quite ready. In fact, everything was as ready as possible. Everything was perfect. But this new maiden looked so beautiful and wealthy, that they felt they had not done enough to prepare. They invited her to join the dance. With a toss of her soft black hair and a bright smile, she stepped into the circle.

The most handsome young men took turns to hold her hand. She laughed and danced with more joy than she had ever felt before. Her feet were light. Her heart was merry. Her breathing grew faster and faster with excitement. She danced until the sun sank low in the western sky.

In all this time, she did not think once of her turkeys. Or if she did think of them, she said to herself, "I will never forget my beloved turkeys. I will dance awhile longer until just before sunset. I want these people to see me and talk for days about the beautiful maiden who came to the dance."

And so she continued to dance. The people would not let her stop. They insisted that she join in every dance. When one dance ended, there was always another. Finally, the sun set and darkness covered the plaza of Zuni.

Suddenly, the beautiful maiden broke away from the dance. Without a word to anyone, she ran out of Zuni and up the path to Salt City. She was used to the hard life on the mountain, and she could run faster than most people. But it was not fast enough.

Waiting in their cages, the turkeys grew restless. "It is just as we expected," said the big gobbler. "Now that her fortune has changed, she has forgotten her turkeys." When the sun had completely set, and Salt City was dark and still, he opened the cage with his beak. He led the other turkeys out, and they walked around the city, opening the other turkey cages. Soon all of the turkeys headed out of Salt City and around the back of Thunder Mountain.

Just then the Turkey Girl arrived. She called to her turkeys to stop. But they ignored her and ran faster, spreading their wings to help them. She chased after them, but they just ran faster singing

a strange old song. They continued through the Gateway of Zuni and up the valley.

Hearing their song, she called again and again. But still they kept on running through Cañon Mesa until they came to the base of the Zuni Mountains. With one last chorus of their song, they spread their wings wide and fluttered up onto the high plains.

Down below, the Turkey Girl watched her beloved turkeys disappear onto the high plains. She threw her hands up in the air and looked down upon her clothing. With the dust of the trail and the sweat of her long run, her clothes looked as dirty and poor as they had looked before. And so she returned to Salt City, sad and alone, without her beloved turkeys.

Today, you can still see the tracks of turkeys in the rocks around Cañon Mesa. There are other figures, too—the song of the turkeys carved in the rocks. People say that there are more wild turkeys on the high plains below the Zuni Mountains than in any other place.

As for the Turkey Girl, her story is sad. But the turkeys believed she got what she deserved. For if we are poor in possessions but rich in our hearts, we deserve the finest things in life. But if we are poor in our hearts, then we deserve to be poor in possessions as well.

The Story Behind This Native American Tale

This tale is based on a story told by the Zuni people. The Zuni live in western New Mexico, close to the Arizona border. When Spanish explorers came to the area in 1540, the Zuni lived in six towns. These towns had buildings with several levels, or stories. The buildings were made of dried earth, wood, and stone. Other Native Americans in the Southwest also lived in towns with similar buildings. The Spanish called these people "Pueblo," which means "town" in Spanish.

The Zuni are the largest of the Pueblo groups, and they speak a language different than the others. Today, about 10,000 people live in Zuni Pueblo, which was built around one of the six old towns. The town that is called "Salt City" in the story was called Mátsaki by the Zuni. It was also one of the six towns, but people no longer live there.

The story of the Turkey Girl was written down by Frank Hamilton Cushing. He lived with the Zuni for over five years, from 1879 to 1885.

Ethnic Tale

The Flower of Life

Not so very long ago a wealthy man and wife had a daughter named Jovita. She was their only child, and they spoiled her. She was good in her heart, but sometimes she had strange ideas. She was used to getting whatever she wanted.

The wealthy family had a servant boy named Manuel, who was raised in their house. Jovita and Manuel were best friends. They did everything together. They played games such as hide-and-seek. They took long walks through the town. They sang songs and laughed at what they sang. They read books and talked about what they read.

In time, Jovita grew into a beautiful young woman, and Manuel became a handsome young man. He loved Jovita. But he was only a servant, so he never told her his feelings.

One year, a terrible illness came to their town, and both of Jovita's parents died. Jovita was now alone in the world. All she had was Manuel. "What shall we do?" she asked him. "My parents died without making a marriage for me." In those days, it was the custom for parents to find their daughters a good husband.

"I don't know," he replied. "It is difficult."

"Wait! I have an idea," she said. "I will have a photograph taken of me. Then I will send copies of the photo to all the princes and kings in the world. Perhaps someone will want to marry me."

Manuel wished that he could marry Jovita himself. But she was a girl from a good family, and he wanted what was best for her. So he agreed that this was a very good idea. Jovita dressed in her finest clothing and had a beautiful picture taken. Manuel helped her send the photo to all the princes and kings in the world.

Years passed, and there was no response to the pictures. Jovita felt very sad. She was already past the age when most girls married in those days. "We need to try something different," she said. She thought and thought, and then she had an idea. "Why don't you marry me, Manuel?"

Manuel was so happy inside that he felt like dancing. This was what he had always wanted. But he still did not show his true feelings. "Why not?" he replied, as if it were a simple question.

Jovita and Manuel were married and lived together in her parents' house. They were happy. They had grown up together. They were best friends. Now they were also husband and wife.

"Oh Manuel, I love you so much," Jovita said one day. "I want us to always be together."

"Of course we will always be together," said Manuel.

"But what if one of us dies?" she asked.

"We will still be together in our hearts," Manuel replied.

Jovita thought for a moment. "Manuel, will you make a bargain with me?"

"Of course," he said. "What kind of bargain?"

"We will both agree that if one of us dies, the one who is alive will be buried with the one who is dead."

Manuel thought this was a strange bargain. But he loved Jovita so much that he agreed. "All right," he said. "Why not?"

It was not long after this that another sickness came to the town and Jovita died. Manuel did not forget their bargain. He had a burial **vault** made of heavy bricks, with a door of iron bars. He placed Jovita's coffin in the vault, and he sat in a chair beside it. A Keeper of the Dead locked the iron door from the outside. Each day, he would slip some food for Manuel through the bars.

Day after day, night after night, Manuel sat beside Jovita's coffin. One day a small mouse crawled under the door and began to eat some crumbs that had dropped from Manuel's plate. Manuel enjoyed having the mouse for company. From then on, he always dropped a few crumbs to feed the mouse. The mouse came and went through the bars of the iron door.

---

vault – a sturdy room or compartment

One day, the mouse brought in a small white flower. Manuel laughed at the sight of the little animal carrying the flower. Without thinking, he picked up a pebble and threw it at the mouse. It struck the little animal in the head, and the mouse fell dead.

"I am so sorry, mouse," said Manuel. "What a foolish thing to do!" He got up from his chair and bent over to pick up the white flower. As he did so, the flower passed across the mouse's nose, and the little animal jumped to its feet alive and well!

Manuel studied the small white flower. It looked like many other flowers. But other flowers did not work magic. "Could this be the flower of life?" he wondered.

He went to Jovita's coffin and opened the lid. Then he passed the flower beneath her nose. "Jovita, my little mouse," he said. "Come alive."

Her lips began to tremble. Still Manuel held the flower beneath her nose. "Please Jovita," he said. "Please smell this flower." Sure enough, she began to breathe and opened her eyes!

"Where are we?" she asked.

Manuel did not want to scare her. So he said, "We are staying at an inn."

Just then the Keeper of the Dead arrived. "With whom are you talking, Manuel?" he asked.

"I am talking with Jovita," Manuel replied.

The Keeper looked at Manuel with pity. He did not know Jovita was alive. "Would you like some food?" he asked.

"No," said Manuel. "Please open this door."

"You know I can't do that," the Keeper explained. "You agreed to the rules."

Manuel went to the door and held out a set of keys. "If you open the door, I will give you some valuable jewels that I left in my chest. Take these keys and go to my house. See for yourself."

The Keeper took the keys and went to the house of Manuel and Jovita. When he returned, he opened the door of the vault. That night, Manuel and Jovita slipped out of the cemetery in the darkness. They kept walking until they came to an inn. There they spent the night. They liked it so much that they decided to stay for a few days, before returning home.

They were still at the inn when Manuel fell sick with a fever. That afternoon, some girls came to the inn and told Jovita that a king had arrived at the shore in a ship. They asked Jovita to join

them. "I would love to go," she replied. "But I can't leave Manuel while he is sick."

Lying in bed, Manuel could hear the girls talking in the other room. "You may go, Jovita," he said. "I will be all right." He did not like the idea of her going. Yet he could never refuse anything Jovita wanted.

Jovita and the girls went down to the shore to see the great ship. The king was standing on the deck in his finest clothes. He held a photograph of Jovita in his hand. Looking at the people who had come to see him, he recognized Jovita and pointed to her. His solders quickly captured her and took her on his ship. Then the ship sailed away.

When the girls told Manuel what had happened, he got up from his bed and went to the shore. He discovered that the king had left orders that anyone who tried to follow him would be killed. Manuel went back to his room and tore his clothes. Then he patched them so he looked like a beggar. He paid the innkeeper to put him into a **barrel** and seal it tightly. The innkeeper rolled the barrel into the ocean.

Manuel floated in the barrel for many days until he came to the other shore. There he smashed his way out of the barrel. He was in a foreign land ruled by the king who had taken Jovita. Manuel stopped at many houses, pretending that he was looking for work. Finally,

barrel – a round container with flat ends and bulging sides

he stopped at the house of an old woman whose son worked in the castle.

"What is your name?" asked the woman.

"Juan Soldado," Manuel replied. This name means "John Soldier" in Spanish.

The old woman then turned to her son. "This nice young man, Juan Soldado, wants to work at the castle. Tell the king that he is your brother who has lived down the coast."

The next day, the woman's son and Manuel went to the king's castle. After hearing the story of the "brother" who lived down the coast, the king hired Juan Soldado as a servant. He was put to work sweeping the kitchen. He wore a big hat to cover his face.

One day, the queen entered the kitchen and noticed the new servant. "What is your name?" she asked.

"Juan Soldado," he replied. He kept his head down and mumbled his words.

The queen stood for a moment looking at the servant. There was something familiar about him. But she could not quite figure it out.

In the days that followed, she visited the kitchen again and again and asked many questions of Juan Soldado. Finally, she realized that it was her real husband, Manuel. That evening the king found her crying.

"My beautiful queen," he said, "why are you so sad?"

"I'm sad because the servant who sweeps our kitchen is my husband."

At this, the king grew very angry. He ordered Manuel into the royal chamber and told him, "Juan Soldado, tonight you will guard three ounces of my gold. If any of the gold is lost, you will be killed."

That night, Manuel guarded the king's gold. But the king tricked him. Two of his servants stole the gold. In the morning, the king ordered Manuel put to death.

While Manuel was in prison, waiting to die, his pretend "brother" visited him. "Listen my friend," said Manuel. "When they kill me you must claim my body. Get a small cart with a fast horse, and put my body in the cart. Take me away from this kingdom. I have a small white flower." Manuel handed the flower of life to his friend. "Once we are out of the kingdom, take this flower and pass it under my nose. Tell me to come alive. Say 'Please Manuel, please come back to life.'"

That evening, Manuel was killed by the king's soldiers. His friend claimed his body and did all that Manuel had told him to do. After Manuel returned to life, his friend took him to the city of the emperor, who was even more powerful than the king. The whole city was sad, because the daughter of the emperor had died that very day.

Manuel went to the palace of the emperor and asked, "Your Majesty, what will you give me if I bring your daughter back to life?"

"I will give you anything you ask," the emperor replied.

"All right," said Manuel. "I ask that you send your army to drive a certain king from his kingdom."

"Your request is granted," said the emperor. "Now bring my daughter back to life."

Manuel went to where the emperor's daughter was lying and passed the flower of life under her nose. "Come alive, my princess," he said. "Please come back to the world of the living." Her lips began to tremble, and soon she

began to breathe. Finally, she opened her eyes and embraced her father!

The emperor's army drove the evil king out of his kingdom, and he was never seen again. Manuel and Jovita are still married and living together happily. Jovita still has strange ideas, and Manuel still tries to give her what she wants. He carefully guards the beautiful flower of life, because he knows they may need it again.

The Story Behind This Ethnic Tale

Most of the American Southwest was once part of Mexico. Texas won independence from Mexico in 1836 and joined the United States in 1845. Arizona and New Mexico became part of the United States in 1848, at the end of the Mexican War. Oklahoma was explored by the Spanish, but it was not part of Mexico.

Today there are many Mexican Americans in the Southwest. Some were born in Mexico. Others have parents, grandparents, or other ancestors who were born in Mexico. There are also people whose ancestors came to the Southwest long ago, when Mexico was ruled by Spain. Many people with family roots in Mexico still speak Spanish, either as a first language or a second language.

This story was written down by Riley Aiken, who was born in Texas near the Mexican border. He heard the story in 1930, told in Spanish by a Mexican-American woman in Marfa, Texas. It is similar in some ways to the fairy tales told in Europe. That is true of many Mexican-American stories.

Regional Tale

Running with the Mustangs

Not that long ago, great herds of wild horses ran free in southern Arizona, near the Mexican border. Wild horses are called mustangs. They were beautiful animals. They had never been ridden. They had never been forced to pull a wagon or a plow. They ran free as the wind through the mountains and desert.

All who saw the mustangs admired their strength and speed and freedom. Two brothers especially liked the horses. These brothers, called Sandiego and Siliaco, were slender and strong. People thought that the brothers walked and acted like horses.

As boys, they would go into the mountains and camp at a little lake where the mustangs drank. They would watch the mustangs carefully from a distance.

"So beautiful and free," said Siliaco.

"So fast and strong," said Sandiego.

Again and again, they came to the mountain lake and watched the mustangs. This went on for years. Just around the time when the boys became grown men, something strange happened in their minds. They began to believe they were horses themselves.

Sandiego was the oldest. By this time he was married, but he had no children. Siliaco, the younger, was single. He had no one but himself to worry about. One day, the two brothers went to the little lake just as a great herd of mustangs thundered into sight. They gazed at the horses in wonder. They imagined that they were horses running with the herd.

"So beautiful and free," said Siliaco.

"So fast and strong," said Sandiego.

Suddenly, without another word, the brothers took off their clothes and ran to join the herd. The horses would run away from any other humans who approached them. But they were not afraid of the brothers. It was as if the horses knew that Sandiego and Siliaco were horses in their minds.

The brothers did not return to their village. They lived with the mustangs. Sometimes people would see them from a distance. The male horse, or stallion, would lead his herd. Behind him came the female horses, or mares, and the young horses, called colts. And finally, at the end came Siliaco and Sandiego.

They galloped and trotted like horses. They snorted and whinnied like horses. They moved their heads to the side and sniffed the air for danger. They threw back their long hair like a horse's mane. They drank from the lake by leaning on their hands and putting their mouths in the water. They truly believed they were wild horses.

At first the brothers stayed together in the same herd. But as time passed, they joined different herds, just like wild horses do. Sometimes Siliaco would go with one herd and Sandiego would go with another. Sometimes they would come back together again.

Once a Mexican cowboy, called a "vaquero," noticed something moving under a palo verde tree. This is a spiny tree with green wood that grows in the deserts and mountains of the Southwest. There were many **vines** growing on the tree, and something was moving behind them. "What kind of animal could this be," the vaquero said to himself. He rode his horse closer to take a look. Suddenly, a wild man with very long hair jumped out of the tree and began to run away. It was Siliaco!

The vaquero had heard of the brothers who ran with the mustangs. So he decided to try and catch him. He rode his horse as fast as he could. Siliaco was a fast runner. But he was not a real horse, of course, and the real horse caught him. The vaquero twirled his rope into a big loop. Then he tossed the loop over Siliaco's shoulders and pulled it tight. Siliaco bucked and whinnied just like a real horse.

The vaquero talked to him quietly and nicely, until Siliaco began to calm down. Gradually, he seemed to return to his human ways. The

---

vine – a plant that grows up a support

vaquero promised to give him food. Siliaco was very hungry, so he agreed to go with the vaquero. He got up on the horse's back, and the two of them rode to the vaquero's camp.

In the camp, the other vaqueros treated Siliaco kindly. They gave him a shirt and pants and shoes. They fed him with good warm beans and meat and tortillas. They gave him hot coffee with sugar. It was difficult for him to speak, because he had been with the horses so long. But his eyes seemed more normal. They thought he might act like a human again.

Siliaco stayed with the vaqueros until they had rounded up all their cattle. Then he followed them to the nearest town. The people of the town also treated Siliaco kindly. He was famous as the man who ran with the mustangs.

Then one night, Siliaco walked out of the town to the edge of the desert. People were always watching him, so a group of men followed to see what he would do. Once he was out of the town, he looked up at the starry sky. Then he sniffed the wind and tilted his head to the side. Perhaps he heard something that the others could not hear. Perhaps he heard the thundering hooves of the mustangs.

Suddenly, Siliaco tore off his clothing and ran into the desert. He ran so swiftly that the others could not catch him.

Siliaco was seen one more time, running with the mustangs. Then he was never seen again. Many years later a traveler made a discovery in

the desert. He found a skeleton of a tall man. Perhaps it was Siliaco.

Sandiego was different. He did not completely forget he was human. Perhaps it was the memory of his wife that brought him back. After a few months he returned to his village and acted like a man again. He and his wife had two sons who grew up to be fine young men. Sandiego was respected by everyone as a good and honest man.

He never spoke of his life among the horses. But he would not ride a horse, and he would not make a horse work. He walked everywhere he went. His steps were very fast, and there was something about his walk that reminded people of a horse. He was a great runner, too. Sandiego lived to be an old man. And even as an old man, he would race against younger men and win.

Still, whenever he had time to spare, he would walk out into the desert. He would stop and sniff the air. He would tilt his head to the side and listen. And then he would gaze into the distance, searching for his brother and the wild mustangs.

The Story Behind This Regional Tale

Between 8,000 and 10,000 years ago, horses became extinct in North America. When an animal becomes "extinct" it means that there are no more animals of that kind. Spanish settlers brought horses from Europe. In 1680, the Pueblo Indians of New Mexico fought against the Spanish and drove them away. The Spanish left behind over three thousand horses.

Horses soon became an important part of life for the Native Americans of the Southwest and West. Over time, some horses escaped or were let free. Soon there were large herds of wild horses, called mustangs. There are still some wild herds of mustangs today.

This tale is based on a story written down by a story collector named J. Frank Dobie. He heard it in Tucson, Arizona in 1951. It was told by a Papago Indian man named Juan Xavier. The Papago live in southern Arizona near the Mexican border. Although the man who told it was Native American, it is not like most Native American stories. It is told as if it really happened a short time ago. Perhaps it did!

Read, Research, and Write

Create a Chart

Does the folktale "The Turkey Girl," remind you of the tale of Cinderella? How are these two stories similar? What makes them different?

- Copy the Venn diagram below.
- Use the diagram to show how the two stories are similar and different.
- Write a note to a friend sharing your ideas about these two stories.

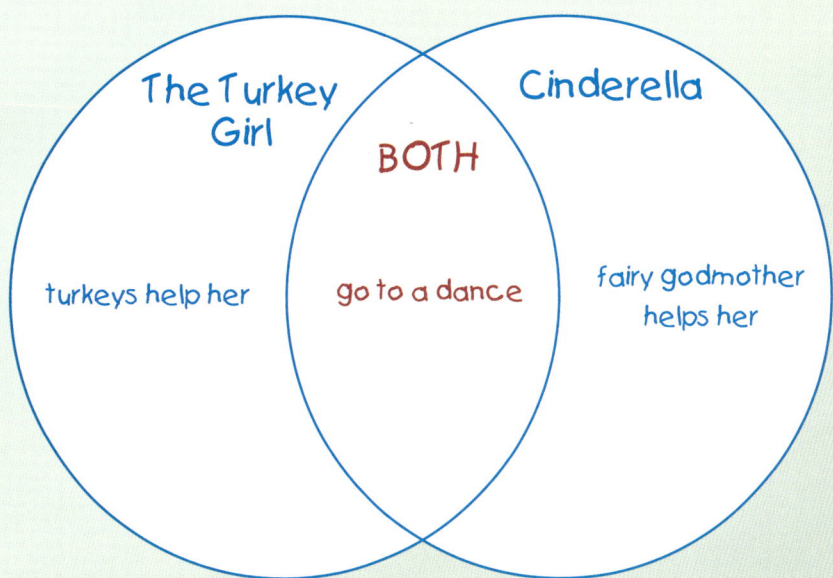

EXTEND YOUR READING

Read More About the Southwest

Find and read more books about the Southwest region of the United States. As you read, think about these questions. They will help you understand more about the topic.

- Who first settled this region?
- What is the climate of the Southwest?
- What sights do visitors go to see in the Southwest?
- What land features are found in the Southwest?

SUGGESTED READING
Reading Expeditions
Travels Across America: The Southwest